A CHEEKY SMILE

Featuring the Nova Babygrow in Pink Glaze (223), Cinder (201) and
Ochre (240) pattern on page 28

Featuring the Bosse Cardigan in
Marine Blue (210) pattern on page 82

LIFE IS FUN WHEN YOU ARE ONE

Featuring the Moses Cable Pants
in Powder Blue (222) pattern on page 78

CONTENTS

INTRODUCTION

MillaMia has always been known for modern baby and children's knitting patterns. This is the first collection for babies and toddlers in the new yarn range Naturally Soft Aran. The quickness of knitting with an aran weight yarn, combined with the softness of the extrafine merino makes for the best of all worlds – super wearable, washable, stylish knits that are quick to produce.

Featuring the Nova Babygrow in Cinder (201), Cobalt (230) and Ochre (240) pattern on page 28

BAREFOOT STYLE

Featuring the Swaddle Kimono in Dusk (220) and Latte (203)
pattern on page 52

While mainly for babies it wouldn't be MillaMia without one or two items for the older kids.

In this collection there is a predominant focus on babies and young toddlers, but as ever where it is appropriate the patterns are graded to allow you to knit them again and again for older children. Many of the items such as the stylish Mona Cardigan look as sophisticated on an 8 year old as they do sweet on a baby.

The nursery pieces span wonderful blankets that make the ideal gift for any newborn, through to the contemporary Folk Cushion in colourwork. The blankets are showcased in a variety of colours – hopefully inspiring you to also be brave in your colour choices. Whatever shades you select the finished item is sure to become an heirloom for the future generation - as suited to their university or college bed as it is to their pram or buggy as they are growing up.

And this is the true beauty of hand knitting – hours invested in producing an item can be considerable, but hours of joy in watching the items worn and used far outweigh the initial effort. Not to mention the pride that any hand knitter feels upon completion of their project.

What differentiates MillaMia patterns from other baby and toddlers knits tends to be our colour palette and sometimes unexpected combinations of colour and design.

Often simple ideas are brought to life with a small change of texture or shade. In this way MillaMia patterns cater for all level of knitter, something easy such as the Freja Blanket – where each square is a quick manageable project in its own right, through to the more complex shaping and colourwork of an item like the Nova Babygrow, which gives the more experienced knitter a challenge to aim for.

Finally you can never go wrong with a hand knitted cardigan for a newborn. There are a bunch to choose from in this book, and it is fun to see how appropriate each style is for both girls and boys. The Swaddle Kimono has such interesting shapes, and the subtle colour changes give a softness that contrasts perfectly with its geometric lines. The Bosse Cardigan is ideal for boys both newborn and older, and the texture gives a gorgeous structured fabric. Enjoy the speed of working your way through this Aran knitting pattern book.

READY TO MAKE TROUBLE

Featuring the Tomas Tank Top in Powder Blue (222) and Ivory (221) pattern on page 88

Top: Folk Cushion in Powder Blue (222) and Ivory (221) pattern on page 74

Bottom: Freja Blanket (folded) in Ivory (221) and Stone (202) pattern on page 64 and the Lapp Blanket in Cinder (201) and Stone (202) pattern on page 48

NURSERY STYLE

The Folk Cushion and Lapp Blanket would make great additions to any baby's nursery. But why limit them to the nursery? Equally as suitable in an adult bedroom or living room. Just choose your colours accordingly.

Featuring the Jens Jumper in
Cinder (201) and Ivory (221)
pattern on page 58

BASIC INFORMATION

SKILL LEVELS

Recognising that we are not all expert knitters we have graded each pattern in the book to allow you to gauge whether it is one that you feel confident to try. The grades are as follows:

Beginner: You have just picked up (or refound) knitting needles and are comfortable with the basic concepts of knitting. By reading carefully you can follow a pattern. Items such as scarves and blankets and simple jumpers are ideal for you to start with.

Beginner / Improving: Having knitted a few pieces you are now looking to try new things, for instance colour combinations and features such as pockets. You might surprise yourself by trying one of the simpler colourwork or cable patterns in this book – you will find that they are not as difficult as you may have thought. Bear in mind that most experienced knitters will be happy to help a beginner. Or look at our website for advice and help.

Improving: You have knitted a variety of items such as jumpers, cardigans and accessories in the past, and are comfortable with following patterns. You may have tried your hand at cable knitting and some form of colourwork before.

Experienced: You are comfortable with most knitting techniques. You have preferences and likes and dislikes, although are willing to try something new. You can read patterns quickly and are able to adapt them to your own requirements – for instance if resizing is needed.

YARN – SOME ADVICE

As there can be colour variations between dye lots when yarn is produced, we suggest that you buy all the yarn required for a project at the same time (with the same dye lot number) to ensure consistency of colour. The amount of yarn required for each pattern is based on average requirements meaning they are an approximate guide.

The designs in this book have been created specifically with a certain yarn composition in mind. The weight, quality, colours, comfort and finished knit effect of this yarn is ideally suited to these patterns. Substituting for another yarn may produce a garment that is different from the design and images in this book.

TENSION / GAUGE

A standard tension is given for all the patterns in this book. As the patterns are in different stitch types (e.g. stocking, garter, rib, etc.) this tension may vary between patterns, and so you must check your tension against the recommendation at the start of the pattern. As matching the tension affects the final shape and size of the item you are knitting it can have a significant impact if it is not matched. Ensuring that you are knitting to the correct tension will result in the beautiful shape and lines of the original designs being achieved.

To check your tension knit a square according to the tension note at the start of each pattern (casting on an additional 10 or more stitches and knitting 5 to 10 more rows than specified in the tension note). You should knit the tension square in the stitch given in the note (e.g. stocking, garter, moss, etc). Once knitted, mark out a 10cm by 10cm / 4in by 4in square using pins and count the number of stitches and rows contained within. If your tension does not quite match the one given try switching to either finer needles (if you have too few stitches in your square) or thicker needles (if you have too many stitches) until you reach the desired tension.

Featuring the Bosse Cardigan in Powder Blue (222) pattern on page 82

15

USEFUL RESOURCES

We believe that using quality trims with our knitwear gives the garments a professional finishing touch. Visit your local yarn/ haberdashery shop for these items and MillaMia yarn or visit www.millamia.com to order yarn directly or find local stockists.

LANGUAGE

This book has been written in UK English. However, where possible US terminology has also been included and we have provided a translation of the most common knitting terms that differ between US and UK knitting conventions on page 20. In addition all sizes and measurements are given in both centimetres and inches throughout. Remember that when a knitting pattern refers to the left and right sides of an item it is referring to the left or right side as worn, rather than as you are looking at it.

SIZES

Alongside the patterns in this book we give measurements for the items – as two children of the same age can have very different measurements, this should be used as a guide when choosing which size to knit. The best way to ensure a good fit is to compare the actual garment measurements given in the pattern with the measurements of an existing garment that fits the child well.

Please note that where a chest measurement is given in the table at the top of each pattern this refers to the total measurement of the garment around the chest. When the cross chest measurement is given graphically in the accompanying diagrams this is half the around chest measurement. Children's clothes are designed with plenty of 'ease', this means that there is not as much shaping or fit to a child's garment as you will find in adult knitwear.

CARE OF YOUR GARMENT

See the ball band of MillaMia Naturally Soft Aran for washing and pressing instructions. Make sure you reshape your garments while they are wet after washing, and dry flat.

READING COLOUR CHARTS

For some of the patterns in this book there are colour charts included. In a colour chart one square represents one stitch and one row. A key shows what each colour in the chart refers to.

The bottom row of the chart indicates the first row of knitting, and as you work your way up, each row of the chart illustrates the next row of knitting. Repeats are the same for all sizes, however different sizes will often require extra stitches as the repeat will not exactly fit. These stitches are marked by vertical lines showing the start and end of rows.

Additional specific instructions are given regarding how to read each chart in the 'Note' at the start of each pattern.

CONFUSED WITH A PATTERN?

The first thing to do is to check the Hints and Tips section in the pattern. In this we include useful additional notes which may answer your query. Or look on our website under the 'Making Knitting Easy' section or our blog if it is a technique query you have.

We check every MillaMia pattern numerous times before we go to print. Despite this occasionally there can be errors in knitting patterns. If you see what you think is an error the best thing is to visit www.millamia.com where any errors that have been spotted will be published under 'Pattern Revisions'. If you cannot find the answer you are looking for, then do send an email (info@millamia.com) or contact us via the website and we will get back to you.

HELLO PRETTY BIRDIE

Featuring the Bee Jumper in Cherry Red (242) and Cinder (201) pattern on page 36

ABBREVIATIONS

alt	alternate
approx	approximately
beg	begin(ning)
cont	continue
dec	decrease(ing)
foll	following
g-st	garter stitch
inc	increase(ing)
k or K	knit
k2 tog	knit two stitches together
m1	make one stitch by picking up the loop lying before the next stitch and knitting into back of it
m1p	make one stitch by picking up the loop lying before the next stitch and purling into back of it
mths	months
p or P	purl
p2 tog	purl two stitches together
patt	pattern
psso	pass slipped stitch over
pwise	purlwise
rib2 tog	rib two stitches together according to rib pattern being followed
rem	remain(ing)
rep	repeat(ing)
skpo	slip one, knit one, pass slipped stitch over – one stitch decreased
sl	slip stitch
st(s)	stitch(es)
st st	stocking stitch
tbl	through back of loop
tog	together
yf	yarn forward
yo	yarn over
yon	yarn over needle to make a st
yrn	yarn round needle
y2rn	wrap the yarn two times around needle. On the following row work into each loop separately working tbl into second loop
[ ]	work instructions within brackets as many times as directed

UK AND US KNITTING TRANSLATIONS

UK	US
Cast off	Bind off
Colour	Color
Grey	Gray
Join	Sew
Moss stitch	Seed stitch
Tension	Gauge
Stocking stitch	Stockinette stitch
Yarn forward	Yarn over
Yarn over needle	Yarn over
Yarn round needle	Yarn over
y2rn	yo2

KNITTING NEEDLE CONVERSION CHART

Metric, mm	US size
2	0
2.25	1
2.5	1
2.75	2
3	2
3.25	3
3.5	4
3.75	5
4	6
4.25	6
4.5	7
5	8
5.5	9
6	10
6.5	10.5
7	10.5
7.5	11
8	11
9	13
10	15

COBALT AND OCHRE - A WINNING COMBINATION

Featuring the Nova Babygrow in Cinder (201), Cobalt (230) and Ochre (240) pattern on page 28

Featuring the Mona Cardigan in Dusk (220) pattern on page 68

22

Featuring the Freja Blanket in
Magenta (232) and Cherry Red (242)
pattern on page 64

NOVA BABYGROW

SKILL LEVEL **Improving**

SIZES / MEASUREMENTS

To fit age	0-3	3-6	6-12	mths

ACTUAL GARMENT MEASUREMENTS

Chest	56	59	61	cm
	22	23	24	in
Length to	45	49	53	cm
shoulder	17 ¾	19 ¼	21	in
Sleeve	14	16	18	cm
length	5 ½	6 ¼	7	in
Inside leg	14	18	21	cm
length	5 ½	7	8 ¼	in

MATERIALS

- 6(7:8) 50g/1 ¾oz balls of MillaMia Naturally Soft Aran in Cinder (201) (M).
- One ball in each of Cobalt (230) (A) and Ochre (240) (B).
- Pair each of 4mm (US 6) and 5mm (US 8) knitting needles.
- 13 buttons approx 15mm/½in in diameter.

TENSION / GAUGE

18 sts and 24 rows to 10cm/4in square over st st using 5mm (US 8) needles.

HINTS AND TIPS

This charming babygrow is a practical way to keep baby warm and cosy as well as being super stylish. The Fairisle elements are a relatively small part of this garment which is a perfect way for the knitter new to Fairisle to try out this colourwork technique. Why not photocopy the chart at a larger size for ease of reading and number each right side row on the right and each wrong side row on the left to remind you which way to begin reading the chart. Remember to maintain an even, not too tight tension over your fairisle section so that it matches the tension on the rest of the garment. Or simply replace with simple stripes if you want something easier.

ABBREVIATIONS

See page 20.

NOTE

When working from Chart odd numbered rows are k rows and read from right to left. Even numbered rows are p rows and read from left to right.

SUGGESTED ALTERNATIVE COLOURWAYS

Pink Glaze	Ochre	Cinder		Latte	Ivory	Marine
223	240	201		203	221	Blue
						210

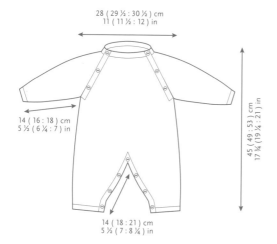

28 (29 ½ : 30 ½) cm
11 (11 ½ : 12) in

14 (16 : 18) cm
5 ½ (6 ¼ : 7) in

45 (49 : 53) cm
17 ¾ (19 ¼ : 21) in

14 (18 : 21) cm
5 ½ (7 : 8 ¼) in

BACK

First leg

With 4mm (US 6) needles and A, cast on 22(24:26) sts.

Rib row [K1, p1] to end.

Rep the last row for 2(3:4)cm/¾(1¼:1½)in, ending with a wrong side row.

Cut off A.

Join on M.

Change to 5mm (US 8) needles.

Beg with a k row cont in st st.

Work 2(4:6) rows.

Inc row K4, m1, k to end.

P 1 row.

Rep the last 2 rows 11 times more, ending with a p row. 34(36:38) sts.

Work 4(8:12) rows.

Shape crotch

Next row Cast off 3 sts, k to end. 31(33:35) sts.

P 1 row.

Leave these sts on a holder.

Second leg

With 4mm (US 6) needles and A, cast on 22(24:26) sts.

Rib row [K1, p1] to end.

Rep the last row for 2(3:4)cm/¾(1¼:1½)in, ending with a wrong side row.

Cut off A.

Join on M.

Change to 5mm (US 8) needles.

Beg with a k row cont in st st.

Work 2(2:4) rows.

Inc row K to last 4 sts, m1, k4.

P 1 row.

Rep the last 2 rows 11 times more, ending with a p row. 34(36:38) sts.

Work 5(9:13) rows.

Shape crotch

Next row Cast off 3 sts, p to end. 31(33:35) sts.

Next row K30(32:34), k last st tog with first st on first leg, k30(32:34). 61(65:69) sts.

Next row P to end.

Next row K26(27:28), skpo, k5(7:9), k2 tog, k26(27:28).

Next row P to end.

Next row K26(27:28), skpo, k3(5:7), k2 tog, k26(27:28).

Next row P to end.

Next row K26(27:28), skpo, k1(3:5), k2 tog, k26(27:28).

2nd and 3rd sizes only

Next row P to end.

Next row K-(27:28), skpo, k-(1:3), k2 tog, k-(27:28).

3rd size only

Next row P to end.

Next row K-(-:28), skpo, k-(-:1), k2 tog, k-(-:28).

All sizes

Next row P to end.

Next row K26(27:28), s1 1, k2 tog, psso, k26(27:28). 53(55:57) sts.

Cont straight until back measures 32(35:38)cm/ 12½(13¾:15)in from cast on edges, ending with a p row **.

Shape armholes

Cast off 3 sts at beg of next 2 rows. 47(49:51) sts.

2nd and 3rd sizes only

Next row Skpo, k to last 2 sts, k2 tog.

Next row P to end.

Rep the last 2 rows -(0:1) times. -(47:47) sts.

All sizes

Cont in patt from Chart.

Mark centre st, then count 23 sts each side of the centre st, this denotes the beg and end of patt. Take into account the decreased sts when working from Chart.

1st row Skpo, patt to last 2 sts, k2 tog.

2nd row Patt to end. 45 sts.

Work the next row in patt, then work 16 rows in M only, then work rows 20 to 24 in patt from Chart, **at the same time**, rep the last 2 rows 11 times. 23 sts.

Cont in M only.

Next row Skpo, k to last 2 sts, k2 tog.

Next row P to end.

Rep the last 2 rows once more and then the dec row again. 17 sts.

Cut off M.

Join on A.

Next row P to end.

Change to 4mm (US 6) needles.

1st rib row P1, [k1, p1] to end.

2nd rib row K1, [p1, k1] to end.

Rep the last 2 rows 1(2:3) times more.

Cast off in rib.

FRONT

Work as given for back to **.

Shape armholes

Cast off 3 sts at beg of **Next 2 rows**. 47(49:51) sts.

2nd and 3rd sizes only

Next row Skpo, k to last 2 sts, k2 tog.

Next row P to end.

Rep the last 2 rows -(0:1) times. -(47:47) sts.

All sizes

Cont in patt from Chart.

Mark centre st, then count 23 sts each side of the centre st, this denotes the beg and end of patt. Take into account the decreased sts when working from Chart.

1st row Skpo, patt to last 2 sts, k2 tog.

2nd row Patt to end. 45 sts.

Work the next 22 rows in patt from Chart, **at the same time**, rep the last 2 rows 11 times. 23 sts.

Cont in M only.

Next row Skpo, k to last 2 sts, k2 tog. 21 sts.

Cut off M.

Join on A.

Next row P to end.

Change to 4mm (US 6) needles.

1st rib row P1, [k1, p1] to end.

2nd rib row K1, [p1, k1] to end.

Rep the last 2 rows 1(2:3) times more.

Cast off in rib.

RIGHT SLEEVE

With 4mm (US 6) needles and A cast on 34(36:38) sts.

Rib row [K1, p1] to end.

Rep the last row for 2(3:4)cm/¾(1¼:1½)in, ending with a wrong side row, inc one st at centre of last row. 35(37:39) sts.

Cut off A.

Join on M.

Change to 5mm (US 8) needles.

Beg with a k row cont in st st.

Work 4 rows.

Inc row K3, m1, k to last 3 sts, m1, k3.

Work 3 rows.

Rep the last 4 rows 4(5:6) times more and then the inc row again. 47(51:55) sts.

Cont straight until sleeve measures 14(16:18)cm/ 5 ½(6 ¼:7)in from cast on edge, ending with a p row. ***.

Shape sleeve top

Next row Cast off 5 sts, k to end.

Next row Cast off 3 sts, p to end. 39(43:47) sts.

2nd and 3rd sizes only

Next row Skpo, k to last 2 sts, k2 tog.

Next row P to end.

Rep the last 2 rows -(0:1) times. -(41:43) sts.

All sizes

Cont in patt from Chart.

Mark centre st, then count 20(21:22) sts to left of the centre st and 18(19:20) sts to the right of centre st, this denotes the beg and end of patt. Take into account the decreased sts when working from Chart.

1st row Skpo, patt to last 2 sts, k2 tog.

2nd row Patt to end. 37(39:41) sts.

Work the next row in patt, then work 16 rows in M only, then work rows 20 to 24 in patt from Chart, **at the same time**, rep the last 2 rows 11 times. 15(17:19) sts.

Cont in M only.

Next row Skpo, k to last 2 sts, k2 tog.

Next row P to last 4 sts, turn.

Next row K to last 2 sts, k2 tog.

Next row P to last 8 sts, turn.

Next row K to last 2 sts, k2 tog. 11(13:15) sts.

Cut off M.

Join on A.

Next row P to end.

Change to 4mm (US 6) needles.

1st rib row P1, [k1, p1] to end.

2nd rib row K1, [p1, k1] to end.

Rep the last 2 rows 1(2:3) times more.

Cast off in rib.

CHART

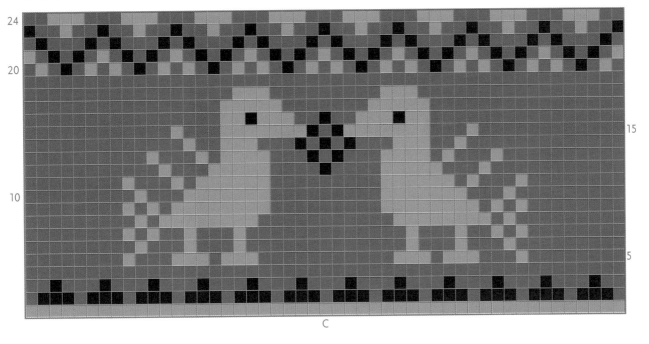

24

20

15

10

5

C

Key
 Cinder (201) (M)
Ochre (240) (B)
Cobalt (230) (A)
C   Centre st

LEFT SLEEVE

Work as given for right sleeve to ***.
Shape sleeve top
Next row Cast off 3 sts, k to end.
Next row Cast off 5 sts, p to end. 39(43:47) sts.
2nd and 3rd sizes only
Next row Skpo, k to last 2 sts, k2 tog.
Next row P to end.
Rep the last 2 rows -(0:1) times. -(41:43) sts.
All sizes
Cont in patt from Chart.
Mark centre st, then count 20(21:22) sts to right of the centre st and 18(19:20) sts to the left of centre st, this denotes the beg and end of patt. Take into account the decreased sts when working from Chart.
1st row Skpo, patt to last 2 sts, k2 tog.
2nd row Patt to end. 37(39:41) sts.
Work the next row in patt, then work 16 rows in M only, then work rows 20 to 24 in patt from Chart, **at the same time**, rep the last 2 rows 11 times. 15(17:19) sts.
Cont in M only.
Next row Skpo, k to last 2 sts, k2 tog.
Next row P to end.
Next row Skpo, k to last 4 sts, turn.
Next row P to end.
Next row Skpo, k to last 8 sts, turn, slip all sts onto left needle. 11(13:15) sts.
Cut off M.
Join on A.
Next row P to end.
Change to 4mm (US 6) needles.
1st rib row P1, [k1, p1] to end.
2nd rib row K1, [p1, k1] to end.
Rep the last 2 rows 1(2:3) times more.
Cast off in rib.

SLEEVE BUTTON BAND (both alike)

With right side facing, using 4mm (US 6) needles and A pick up and k23(25:27) sts evenly along front sleeve edge.
1st rib row P1, [k1, p1] to end.
2nd rib row K1, [p1, k1] to end.
Rep the first row again.
Cast off in rib.

FRONT BUTTONHOLE BAND (both alike)

With right side facing, using 4mm (US 6) needles and A pick up and k23(25:27) sts evenly along front raglan edge.
1st rib row P1, [k1, p1] to end.
This row sets the rib.
Buttonhole row Rib 4, yrn, rib2 tog, [rib 5(6:7), yrn, rib2 tog] twice, rib 3.
Rib 1 more row.
Cast off in rib.

LEG BUTTON BAND

Join cast off edges to form crotch seam.
With right side facing, using 4mm (US 6) needles and A pick up and k59(67:75) sts evenly along back leg edges.
1st rib row P1, [k1, p1] to end.
2nd rib row K1, [p1, k1] to end.
Rep the last 2 rows once more and then the first row again.
Cast off in rib.

LEG BUTTONHOLE BAND

With right side facing, using 4mm (US 6) needles and A pick up and k59(67:75) sts evenly along front leg edges.
1st rib row P1, [k1, p1] to end.
2nd rib row K1, [p1, k1] to end.
Buttonhole row Rib 5(6:7), yrn, rib2 tog, [rib 6(7:8), yrn rib 2 tog] 3 times, rib 6(7:8), rib2 tog, yrn, [rib 6(7:8), rib2 tog, yrn] twice, rib 4(5:6).
Rib 2 more rows.
Cast off in rib.

TO MAKE UP

Join side and sleeve seams. Join back raglan seams. Join under arm seam. Lap buttonhole band over buttonband and sew in place. Sew on buttons.

BEE JUMPER

SKILL LEVEL **Beginner / Improving**

SIZES / MEASUREMENTS

To fit age	0-3	3-6	6-12	12-24	24-36	36-48	mths

ACTUAL GARMENT MEASUREMENTS

Chest	43	48	52	56	61	65	cm
	17	19	20 ½	22	24	25 ½	in
Length to	23	25	28	31	34	38	cm
shoulder	9	10	11	12 ¼	13 ½	15	in
Sleeve	13	15	17	19	22	25	cm
length	5	6	6 ¾	7 ½	8 ¾	9 ½	in

MATERIALS

• 2(3:3:4:4:5) 50g/ 1 ¾oz balls each of MillaMia Naturally Soft Aran in Ochre (240) (M) and 2(2:2:3:3:3) balls in Slate (200) (A).
• Pair each of 4.5mm (US 7) and 5mm (US 8) knitting needles.

TENSION / GAUGE

18 sts and 24 rows to 10cm/4in square over st st using 5mm (US 8) needles.

HINTS AND TIPS

The simple construction of this sweater makes it the perfect project for a beginner who wants to challenge themselves by adding colour stripes and a little bit of shaping. To produce a neat finish on the 'wrap and turn' sections it is a good idea to pick up the wraps on the returning row when you reach them. They are easily recognisable – the 'wrap' looks like a horizontal bar across the bottom of the stitch. On a knit row pick up the wrap with your right needle and place it onto the left alongside the stitch it was wrapping and then knit the 2 stitches together. Although it is not essential to pick up and knit the wraps, it does erase them and produces the smoothest finish.

ABBREVIATIONS

See page 20.

NOTE

To 'wrap 1' -
on k rows: yarn to front, sl st to be wrapped pwise from left needle to right, yarn to back, sl st back from right to left needle, turn.
on p rows: yarn to back, sl st to be wrapped pwise from left needle to right, yarn to front, sl st back from right to left needle, turn.

SUGGESTED ALTERNATIVE COLOURWAYS

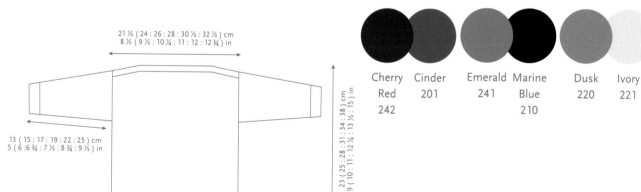

Cherry Red 242   Cinder 201   Emerald 241   Marine Blue 210   Dusk 220   Ivory 221

21 ½ (24 : 26 : 28 : 30 ½ : 32 ½) cm
8 ½ (9 ½ : 10 ¼ : 11 : 12 : 12 ¾) in

13 (15 : 17 : 19 : 22 : 25) cm
5 (6 : 6 ¾ : 7 ½ : 8 ¾ : 9 ½) in

23 (25 : 28 : 31 : 34 : 38) cm
9 (10 : 11 : 12 ¼ : 13 ½ : 15) in

BACK and FRONT (alike)

With 5mm (US 8) needles and M cast on 41(45:49:53:57:61) sts.
Beg with a k row work in st st.
Work 10(10:12:12:14:14) rows.
Cont in stripes of 6(7:8:8:10:11) rows A, [6(7:8:8:10:11) rows M, 6(7:8:8:10:11) rows A] twice, then cont in M only until work measures 23(25:28:31:34:38)cm/9(10:11:12 ¼:13 ½:15)in from cast on edge, ending with a p row.

Shape shoulders

Next 2 rows K to last 4 sts, wrap 1, turn, p to last 4 sts, wrap 1, turn.

Next 2 rows K to last 8 sts, wrap 1, turn, p to last 8 sts, wrap 1, turn.

Next row K to end.
Change to 4.5mm (US 7) needles.
K 4 rows.

Next row K7(8:9:10:11:12), cast off next 27(29:31:33:35:37) sts, k to end.
Leave both sets of sts on a spare needle.

SLEEVES

With 4.5mm (US 7) needles and A cast on 21(23:25:27:29:31) sts.
K7(7:7:9:9:9) rows.
Change to 5mm (US 8) needles.
Beg with a k row work in st st and stripes of [6(7:8:8:10:11) rows M, 6(7:8:8:10:11) rows A] twice, then cont in M only. At the same time:
Work 4 rows.

Inc row K3, m1, k to last 3 sts, m1, k3.
Work 3 rows.
Rep the last 4 rows 4(5:6:7:9:10) times more and then the inc row again. 33(37:41:43:49:53) sts.
Cont straight until sleeve measures 13(15:17:19:22:24)cm/ 5(6:6 ¾:7 ½: 8 ¾:9 ½)in from cast on edge, ending with a p row.

Shape sleeve top
Cast off 4 sts at beg of next 6 rows. Cast off.

TO MAKE UP

With needles pointing in the same direction and right sides together, cast off shoulder sts together. Sew on sleeves. Join side and sleeve seams.

TIPPEN SOCKS

SIZES
To fit age   0-6   6-18   24-48   mths

MATERIALS
• One 50g/1 ¾oz ball each of MillaMia Naturally Soft Aran in Cinder (201) (A) and Ochre (240) (B).
• Pair each of 4mm (US 6) and 4.5mm (US 7) knitting needles.

TENSION / GAUGE
21 sts and 27 rows to 10cm/4in over st st using 4.5mm (US 7) needles.

HINTS AND TIPS
These chunky, colour block socks are perfect paired with a co-ordinating Toppen Hat to keep a stylish baby warm and snug from head to toe. Knitted flat and seamed at the back, these socks are also a great introduction to the simple shaping techniques required to knit socks.

ABBREVIATIONS
See page 20.

SUGGESTED ALTERNATIVE COLOURWAYS

Marine Blue 210   Emerald 241   Cherry Red 242   Latte 203   Magenta 232   Slate 200

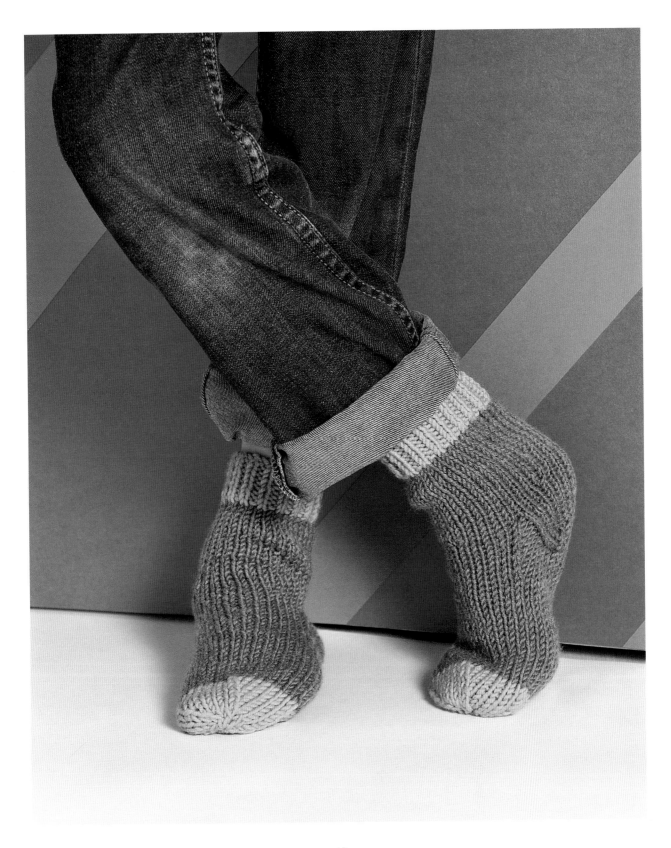

TO MAKE

With 4mm (US 6) needles and B cast on 32(36:40) sts.
Rib row [K1, p1] to end.
Rib a further 3(5:7) rows.
Cut off B.
Change to 4.5mm (US 7) needles and A.
Beg with a k row, cont in st st.
Work 2(2:4) rows.
Dec row K5, k2 tog, k to last 7 sts, skpo, k5.
Work 3(5:7) rows.
Dec row K4, k2 tog, k to last 6 sts, skpo, k4.
Work 3(3:5) rows.
Dec row K2(3:3), [k2 tog, k5(6:7)] twice, skpo, k5(6:7), skpo, k3(3:4). 24(28:32) sts.

Shape heel

Next row P7(8:9) sts only, turn.
Work 9 rows in st st on these 7(8:9) sts only.
Dec row P1(2:3), p2 tog, p1, turn.
Next row Sl 1, k2(3:4).
Dec row P2(3:4), p2 tog, p1, turn.
Next row Sl 1, k3(4:5).
Dec row P3(4:5), p2 tog.
Leave rem 4(5:6) sts on a holder.
With wrong side facing, slip centre 10(12:14) sts onto a holder, rejoin yarn to rem 7(8:9) sts, p to end.
Work 8 rows in st st on these 7(8:9) sts.
Dec row K1(2:3), skpo, k1, turn.
Next row Sl 1, p2(3:4).
Dec row K2(3:4), skpo, k1, turn.
Next row Sl 1, p3(4:5).
Dec row K3(4:5), skpo, turn.
Next row Sl 1, p3(4:5).

Shape instep

Next row K4(5:6), pick up and k8 sts evenly along inside edge of heel, k10(12:14) sts from holder, pick up and k8 sts along inside edge of heel and k4(5:6) sts from holder. 34(38:42) sts.
P 1 row.
Dec row K10(11:12), k2 tog, k10(12:14), skpo, k10(11:12).
P 1 row.
Dec row K9(10:11), k2 tog, k10(12:14), skpo, k9(10:11).
P 1 row.
Dec row K8(9:10), k2 tog, k10(12:14), skpo, k8(9:10).
P 1 row.
Dec row K7(8:9), k2 tog, k10(12:14), skpo, k7(8:9).
26(30:34) sts.
Work 9(13:17) rows straight.
Cut off A.
Change to B.

Shape toe

Dec row K1, [skpo, k4(5:6)] 4 times, k1.
P 1 row.
Dec row K1, [skpo, k3(4:5)] 4 times, k1.
P 1 row.
Dec row K1, [skpo, k2(3:4)] 4 times, k1.
P 1 row.
Dec row K1, [skpo, k1(2:3)] 4 times, k1.
Dec row [P2 tog tbl] 5(7:9) times.
Break off yarn, thread through rem sts, pull up and secure.
Join seam.

TOPPEN HAT

SKILL LEVEL **Beginner / Improving**

SIZES / MEASUREMENTS

To fit age   6-12   12-24   36-48   mths

ACTUAL GARMENT MEASUREMENTS

Round	34	39	44	cm
head	13 ½	15 ½	17 ½	in

MATERIALS

• One 50g/1 ¾oz ball MillaMia Naturally Soft Aran in each of Magenta (232) (A) and Slate (200) (B).
• One pair of 5mm (US 8) knitting needles.

TENSION / GAUGE

18 sts and 24 rows to 10cm/4in square over st st using 5mm (US 8) needles.

HINTS AND TIPS

This cute hat is a really quick knit and can be easily personalised by choice of contrasting colours and the size of pom pom. We used a pom pom maker to make a 6cm/2 ½in pom pom for the hat shown in the picture, but you could make a smaller pom pom if preferred. See the Tippen Socks pattern to make coordinating socks to keep baby warm and cosy from head to toe.

ABBREVIATIONS

See page 20.

SUGGESTED ALTERNATIVE COLOURWAYS

Cinder 201   Ochre 240   Cherry Red 242   Latte 203   Emerald 241   Marine Blue 210

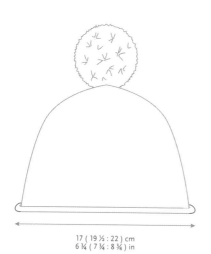

17 (19 ½ : 22) cm
6 ¾ (7 ¾ : 8 ¾) in

TO MAKE

Using 5mm (US 8) needles and A cast on 64(73:82) sts.
Starting with a k row work 38(42:46) rows st st.
Break off A. Join on B.
Dec row K1, [k2 tog, k7] 7(8:9) times. 57(65:73) sts.
P 1 row.
Dec row K1, [k2 tog, k6] 7(8:9) times. 50(57:64) sts.
P 1 row.
Dec row K1, [k2 tog, k5] 7(8:9) times. 43(49:55) sts.
P 1 row.
Dec row K1, [k2 tog, k4] 7(8:9) times. 36(41:46) sts.
P 1 row.
Dec row K1, [k2 tog, k3] 7(8:9) times. 29(33:37) sts.
P 1 row.
Dec row K1, [k2 tog, k2] 7(8:9) times. 22(25:28) sts.
P 1 row.
Next row K0(1:0), [k2 tog] to end. 11(13:14) sts.
Next row P1(1:0), [p2 tog] to end. 6(7:7) sts.
Break off yarn, thread through rem sts, pull up and secure.

TO MAKE UP

Join seam, reversing seam on the roll of the hem.
Using B, make a large pompon and attach to top of hat.

LAPP BLANKET

SKILL LEVEL **Beginner / Improving**

MEASUREMENTS
Approx 78cm/30 ¾in by 78cm/30 ¾in.

MATERIALS
Two colour version
• Eight 50g/1 ¾oz balls of MillaMia Naturally Soft Aran in Cinder (201) (M).
• Six balls in Stone (202) (C).

One colour version
• Thirteen 50g/1 ¾oz balls of MillaMia Naturally Soft Aran in Latte (203).

All versions
• Pair each of 4mm (US 6) and 5mm (US 8) needles.
• Cable needle.

TENSION / GAUGE
18 sts and 24 rows to 10cm/4in square over st st using 5mm (US 8) needles.

HINTS AND TIPS
A handknitted blanket gifted to a newborn is always truly well received, and this warm and cosy cover will be no exception. Due to the multi-block design, this blanket can be knitted in bite-sized pieces making it easily achievable, size adaptable, and of course the perfect 'travel project'.

ABBREVIATIONS
C8F, cable 8 front - slip next 4 sts on a cable needle and hold at front of work, k4, then k4 from cable needle.
C8B, cable 8 back - slip next 4 sts on a cable needle and hold at back of work, k4, then k4 from cable needle.
C4F, cable 4 front - slip next 2 sts on a cable needle and hold at front of work, k2, then k2 from cable needle.
C4B, cable 4 back - slip next 2 sts on a cable needle and hold at back of work, k2, then k2 from cable needle.
See also page 20.

SUGGESTED ALTERNATIVE COLOURWAYS

Stone	Pink Glaze	Teal	Damson	Cobalt	Powder Blue
202	223	231	233	230	222

78 cm / 30 ¾ in

78 cm / 30 ¾ in

TO MAKE (make 16)

If making the single colour version knit 16 squares in total. If making the two colour version knit 8 in each colour.

With 5mm (US 8) needles leaving 30cm/12in for sewing up cast on 38 sts.

1st row P4, k4, p3, k16, p3, k4, p4.

2nd row P to end.

3rd row P4, C4F, p3, k4, [slip next 4 sts on a cable needle and hold at front of work, inc in each of next 2 sts, k4 from cable needle] twice, p3, C4B, p4. 42 sts.

4th row P to end.

Work in main patt.

1st row P4, k4, p3, k20, p3, k4, p4.

2nd row and every wrong side row P to end.

3rd row P4, C4F, p3, k20, p3, C4B, p4.

5th row As 1st row.

7th row P4, C4F, p3, [C8B] twice, k4, p3, C4B, p4.

9th row As 1st row.

11th row P4, C4F, p3, k20, p3, C4B, p4.

13th row As 1st row.

15th row P4, C4F, p3, k4, [C8F] twice, p3, C4B, p4.

16th row P to end.

These 16 rows form the patt.

Work a further 30 rows.

Dec row P4, C4F, p3, k4, * slip next 4 sts onto a cable needle and hold at front of work, k2, [slip 1 from cable needle, k next st from left hand needle, psso] twice, then k last 2 sts on cable needle *; rep from * to * once more, p3, C4B, p4.

Next row P to end.

Leaving 30cm/12in for sewing up cast off.

TO MAKE UP

Alternating the colours and direction of the squares, make up the squares to form a blanket 4 squares wide by 4 squares deep.

EDGING (work 4 sides separately)

With right side facing, using 4mm (US 6) needles and M, pick up and k152 sts along side.

1st row K to end.

2nd row K1, m1, k to last st, m1, k1.

Rep the last 2 rows 4 times more.

Cast off.

Join row ends to form mitres.

SWADDLE KIMONO

SKILL LEVEL **Beginner / Improving**

SIZES / MEASUREMENTS

To fit age	0-3	3-6	6-9	9-12	12-18	18-24	mths

ACTUAL GARMENT MEASUREMENTS

Chest	46	51	55	60	64	69	cm
	18	20	21 ½	23 ½	25	27	in
Length to	26	28	30	33	36	38	cm
back neck	10 ¼	11	11 ¾	13	14	15	in
Sleeve	6	9	11	13	15	18	cm
length	2 ¼	3 ½	4 ¼	5	6	7	in
(with cuff turned back)							

MATERIALS

- 3(4:4:5:5) 50g/1 ¾oz balls of MillaMia Naturally Soft Aran in Latte (203) (M).
- 2(2:3:3:4) balls in Pink Glaze (223) (C).
- Pair each of 4.5mm (US 7) and 5mm (US 8) knitting needles.
- Circular 5mm (US 8) needle.
- 4 buttons approx 21mm/¾in in diameter.

TENSION / GAUGE

18 sts and 24 rows to 10cm/4in square over st st using 5mm (US 8) needles.

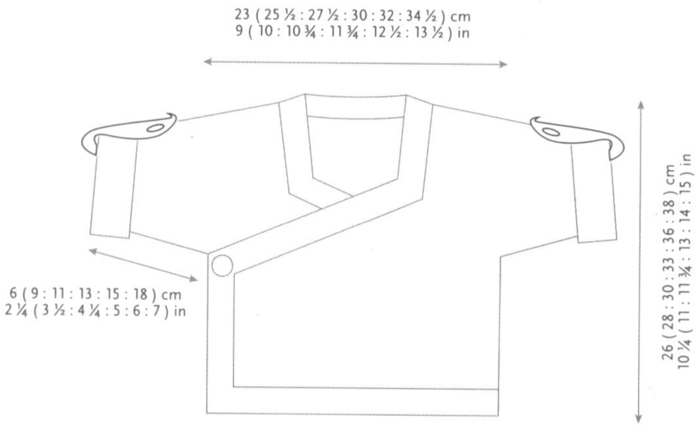

HINTS AND TIPS

The simple shape of this kimono style cardigan makes it a comfortable, easy piece for babies to wear. A neutral shape makes it suitable for boys and girls alike and can be easily made more gender specific (if required) with choice of colour. To produce a neat finish on the 'wrap and turn' sections it is a good idea to pick up the wraps on the returning row when you reach them. They are easily recognizable – the 'wrap' looks like a horizontal bar across the bottom of the stitch. On a knit row, pick up the wrap with your right needle and place it onto the left alongside the stitch it was wrapping and then knit the 2 stitches together. Although it is not essential to pick up and knit the wraps, it does erase them and produces the smoothest finish.

ABBREVIATIONS

See page 20.

NOTE

To 'wrap 1' -
on k rows: yarn to front, sl st to be wrapped pwise from left needle to right, yarn to back, sl st back from right to left needle, turn.
on p rows: yarn to back, sl st to be wrapped pwise from left needle to right, yarn to front, sl st back from right to left needle, turn.

SUGGESTED ALTERNATIVE COLOURWAYS

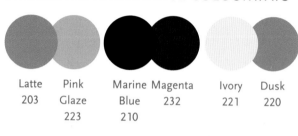

Latte 203   Pink Glaze 223   Marine Blue 210   Magenta 232   Ivory 221   Dusk 220

23 (25 ½ : 27 ½ : 30 : 32 : 34 ½) cm
9 (10 : 10 ¾ : 11 ¾ : 12 ½ : 13 ½) in

6 (9 : 11 : 13 : 15 : 18) cm
2 ¼ (3 ½ : 4 ¼ : 5 : 6 : 7) in

26 (28 : 30 : 33 : 36 : 38) cm
10 ¼ (11 : 11 ¾ : 13 : 14 : 15) in

BACK and SLEEVES (worked in one piece)

With 4.5mm (US 7) needles and M cast on
44(48:52:56:60:64) sts.
K 11(11:13:13:15:15) rows.
Change to 5mm (US 8) needles.
Beg with a k row work in stripes of 2 rows C and 2 rows M.
Work 20(24:26:30:34:38) rows st st.
Change to 5mm (US 8) circular needle.

Shape sleeves
Cast on 3(4:5:6:7:8) sts at beg of next 8 rows.
68(80:92:104:116:128) sts.
Work a further 18(20:22:24:26:28) rows.
Shape upper sleeve and shoulders
Next 2 rows K to last 3(4:5:6:7:8) sts, wrap 1, turn, p to
last 3(4:5:6:7:8) sts, wrap 1, turn.
Next 2 rows K to last 6(8:10:12:14:16) sts, wrap 1, turn, p to
last 6(8:10:12:14:16) sts, wrap 1, turn.
Next 2 rows K to last 9(12:15:18:21:24) sts, wrap 1, turn, p to
last 9(12:15:18:21:24) sts,wrap 1, turn.
Next 2 rows K to last 12(16:20:24:28:32) sts, wrap 1, turn, p to
last 12(16:20:24:28:32) sts, wrap 1, turn.
Next 2 rows K to last 26(31:36:41:46:51) sts, wrap 1, turn, p to
last 26(31:36:41:46:51) sts, wrap 1, turn.
Leave centre 16(18:20:22:24:26) sts on a holder.

LEFT FRONT and SLEEVE

With 4.5mm (US 7) needles and M cast on
44(48:52:56:60:64) sts.
K 11(11:13:13:15:15) rows.
Change to 5mm (US 8) needles.
1st row K40(44:48:52:56:60)C, k4M.
2nd row K4M, p40(44:48:52:56:60)C.
3rd row Using M, k to end.
4th row Using M, k4, p to end.
These 4 rows form the st st stripes with g-st edging.
Work a further 16(20:22:26:30:34) rows.
Change to 5mm (US 8) circular needle.

Shape sleeve and front neck
Next row Cast on 3(4:5:6:7:8) sts, k to last 6 sts, place these
6 sts on a holder.
Next row P to end.
Next row Cast on 3(4:5:6:7:8) sts, k to last 3 sts, place these
3 sts on same holder.
Next row P to end.
Rep the last 2 rows twice more.
Next row K to last 3 sts, place these 3 sts on same holder.
Next row P to end.
Rep the last 2 rows 4(5:6:7:8:9) times more.
There are now 30(33:36:39:42:45) sts on the holder.
Work a further 8 rows.
Shape upper sleeve and shoulder
Next 2 rows K to end, turn, p to last 3(4:5:6:7:8) sts,
wrap 1, turn.
Next 2 rows K to end, turn, p to last 6(8:10:12:14:16) sts,
wrap 1, turn.
Next 2 rows K to end, turn, p to last 9(12:15:18:21:24) sts,
wrap 1, turn.
Next 2 rows K to end, turn, p to last 12(16:20:24:28:32) sts,
wrap 1, turn.
Next row K to end.
Leave these 26(31:36:41:46:51) sts on a spare needle.

RIGHT FRONT and SLEEVE

With 4.5mm (US 7) needles and M cast on
44(48:52:56:60:64) sts.
K 11(11:13:13:15:15) rows.
Change to 5mm (US 8) needles.
1st row K4M, 40(44:48:52:56:60)C.
2nd row P40(44:48:52:56:60)C, k4M.
3rd row Using M, k to end.
4th row Using M, p to last 4 sts, k4.
These 4 rows form the st st stripes with g-st edging.
Work a further 16(20:22:26:30:34) rows.
Change to 5mm (US 8) circular needle.
Shape sleeve and front neck
Next row K1, k2 tog, yf, k3 sts, place these 6 sts on a holder, k to end.
Next row Cast on 3(4:5:6:7:8) sts, p last 3 sts, place these 3 sts on same holder.
Next row K to end.
Next row Cast on 3(4:5:6:7:8) sts, p to last 3 sts, place these 3 sts on same holder.
Rep the last 2 rows twice more.
Next row K to end.
Next row P to last 3 sts, place these 3 sts on same holder.
Rep the last 2 rows 3(4:5:6:7:8) times more.
There are now 30(33:36:39:42:45) sts on the holder.
Work a further 8 rows.
Shape upper sleeve and shoulder
Next 2 rows K to last 3(4:5:6:7:8) sts, wrap 1, turn, p to end.
Next 2 rows K to last 6(8:10:12:14:16) sts, wrap 1, turn, p to end.
Next 2 rows K to last 9(12:15:18:21:24) sts, wrap 1, turn, p to end.
Next 2 rows K to last 12(16:20:24:28:32) sts, wrap 1, turn, p to end.
Leave these 26(31:36:41:46:51) sts on a spare needle.

FRONT EDGING

Places sts for back and two front shoulder and upper sleeves on needles pointing in the same direction, with right sides facing, cast these sts off together to form a seam.
With right side facing, starting at right front neck edge, using 4.5mm (US 7) needles and M, place 6 sts on a needle, k24(27:30:33:36:39), pick up and k18 sts up right front to shoulder, k16(18:20:22:24:26) from back neck holder, pick up and k18 sts down left front neck edge, k27(30:33:36:39:42), yf, k2 tog, k1 from left front holder.
K 6 rows.
Cast off.

CUFFS

With wrong side facing, using 4.5mm (US 7) needles and M, pick up and k30(34:38:42:46:50) sts along row ends.
K14 rows.
Cast off.

SLEEVE BUTTONHOLE BAND (make 2)

With 4.5mm (US 7) needles and M cast on 20(20:22:22:24:24) sts.
K 5 rows.
Buttonhole row K3, k2 tog, yf, k to end.
K 6 rows.
Cast off.

TO MAKE UP

Join side and sleeve seams. Sew cast on edge of sleeve buttonhole band to back of picked up sts of cuff on shoulder seam. Fold back cuffs. Sew on buttons.

JENS JUMPER

SKILL LEVEL **Improving**

SIZES / MEASUREMENTS

To fit age	3-6	6-12	12-24	24-36	36-48	mths

ACTUAL GARMENT MEASUREMENTS

Chest	54	61	68	74	81	cm
	21 ¼	24	26 ¾	29	32	in
Length to	24	28	32	37	42	cm
shoulder	9 ½	11	12 ½	14 ½	16 ½	in
Sleeve	14	16	19	22	25	cm
length	5 ½	6 ¼	7 ½	8 ¾	9 ¾	in

MATERIALS

• 3 (4:4:5:6) 50g/1 ¾oz balls of MillaMia Naturally Soft Aran in Cinder (201) (M).
• Two balls in Ivory (221) (C).
• Pair each of 4mm (US 6) and 5mm (US 8) knitting needles.

TENSION / GAUGE

18 sts and 24 rows to 10cm/4in square over st st using 5mm (US 8) needles.

HINTS AND TIPS

This unisex jumper is an easy to wear piece that will look super fun paired with jeans or a cute skirt. The fairisle section on the front is easily managed in just 2 colours. To accomodate the pattern the jumper ends up being a loose, relatively boxy fit.

ABBREVIATIONS

See page 20.

NOTE

When working from Chart odd numbered rows are k rows and read from right to left. Even numbered rows are p rows and read from left to right.

SUGGESTED ALTERNATIVE COLOURWAYS

Powder Blue 222   Cinder 201   Magenta 232   Stone 202   Marine Blue 210   Ivory 221

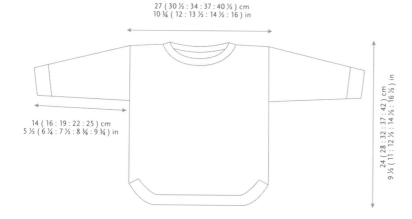

27 (30 ½ : 34 : 37 : 40 ½) cm
10 ¾ (12 : 13 ½ : 14 ½ : 16) in

14 (16 : 19 : 22 : 25) cm
5 ½ (6 ¼ : 7 ½ : 8 ¾ : 9 ¾) in

24 (28 : 32 : 37 : 42) cm
9 ½ (11 : 12 ½ : 14 ½ : 16 ½) in

BACK

With 5mm (US 8) needles and M, cast on 37(43:47:51:55) sts.
Beg with a k row cont in st st.
Work 2 rows.
Inc row K1, m1, k to last st, m1, k1.
Next row P to end.
Rep the last 2 rows 2(2:3:4:5) times more.
Cast on 4 sts at beg of next 2 rows. 51(57:63:69:75) sts.
Beg with a k row work in st st until back measures
22(26:30:35:40)cm/8 ¾(10 ¼:11 ¾:13 ¾:15 ¾)in from cast on
edge, ending with a p row.
Shape back neck
Next row K17(19:21:23:25), turn and work on these sts.
Dec one st at neck edge on next 4 rows. 13(15:17:19:21) sts.
Work 1 row.
Shape shoulder
Cast off 6(7:8:9:10) sts at the beg of next row.
Work 1 row.
Cast off rem 7(8:9:10:11) sts.
With right side facing slip centre 17(19:21:23:25) sts on a
holder, rejoin yarn to rem sts, k to end.
Dec one st at neck edge on next 4 rows. 13(15:17:19:21) sts.
Work 2 rows.

Shape shoulder
Cast off 6(7:8:9:10) sts at the beg of next row.
Work 1 row.
Cast off rem 7(8:9:10:11) sts.

FRONT

Work as given for back until front measures 8(11:14:19:23)cm/
3 ¼(4 ½:5 ½:7 ½:9)in from cast on edge, ending with a p row.
Work in patt from Chart.
Using M, work 2 rows.
Shape front neck
Next row K20(22:24:26:28), turn and work on these sts.
Dec one st at neck edge on next 7 rows.
13(15:17:19:21) sts.
Work a few rows straight until front measures the same as
back to shoulder, ending at armhole edge.
Shape shoulder
Cast off 6(7:8:9:10) sts at the beg of next row.
Work 1 row.
Cast off rem 7(8:9:10:11) sts.
With right side facing slip centre 11(13:15:17:19) sts on a
holder, rejoin yarn to rem sts, k to end.
Dec one st at neck edge on next 7 rows.
13(15:17:19:21) sts.

CHART

1st size
2nd size
3rd size
4th size
5th size

Key
■ Cinder (201) (M)
□ Ivory (221) (C)

Work a few rows straight until front measures the same as back to shoulder, ending at armhole edge.

Shape shoulder

Cast off 6(7:8:9:10) sts at the beg of next row.

Work 1 row.

Cast off rem 7(8:9:10:11) sts.

SLEEVES

With 4mm (US 6) needles and C cast on 30(32:34:36:38) sts.

Rib row [K1, p1] to end.

Rep the last row 7(7:9:9:11) times.

Cut off C.

Join on M.

Change to 5mm (US 8) needles.

Starting with a k row, work 2 rows in st st.

Inc row K3, m1, k to last 3 sts, m1, k3.

Work 3 rows.

Rep the last 4 rows 4(5:6:8:10) times and then the inc row again. 42(46:50:56:62) sts.

Cont straight until sleeve measures 14(16:19:22:25) cm/
5 ½(6 ¼:7 ½:8 ¾:9 ¾)in from cast on edge, ending with a p row.

Cast off.

NECKBAND

Join right shoulder seam.

With 4mm (US 6) needles, right side facing, and C pick up and k12(14:16:18:20) sts
down left side of front neck, k11(13:15:17:19) sts on front neck holder, pick up and k12(14:16:18:20) sts up right side of front neck, 8 sts down right side of back neck, k17(19:21:23:25) sts on back neck holder, pick up and k8 sts up left side of back neck. 68(76:84:92:100) sts.

Rib row [K1, p1] to end.

Rep the last row 5 times.

Cast off loosely in rib.

LOWER BORDER (both alike)

With 4mm (US 6) needles and C beg at top of shaped edge, with right side facing, pick up and k10(10:12:14:16) sts down slope, 35(41:45:51:55) along bottom and 10(10:12:14:16) up slope on other side.

1st row (wrong side) [K1, p1] 4(4:5:6:7) times, inc in each of next 4 sts, k1, [p1, k1] 15(18:20:23:25) times, inc in each of next 4 sts, [p1, k1] 4(4:5:6:7) times.

Rib 5 rows as set.

Cast off in rib.

TO MAKE UP

Join left shoulder and neckband seam. Join side and sleeve seams. Sew in sleeves. Sew row ends of lower border to cast on sts on body.

FREJA BLANKET

SKILL LEVEL **Beginner**

MEASUREMENTS
Approx 70cm/27 ½in by 70cm/27 ½in.

MATERIALS
• Six 50g/1 ¾oz balls each of MillaMia Naturally Soft Aran in Ivory (221) (A).
• Three balls in Stone (202) (B).
• Pair each of 4mm (US 6) and 5mm (US 8) knitting needles.

TENSION / GAUGE
18 sts and 24 rows to 10cm/4in square over st st using 5mm (US 8) needles.

HINTS AND TIPS
This is a great pattern to adapt and personalise. Creating a large knitted item from smaller elements is always the best way to make it achievable, but is also an excellent basis for adding in extra colour and differing the stripe pattern to make it truly unique. If you add extra squares to make the blanket larger, remember that you will need to knit a proportional amount to keep the square shape e.g instead of 4 x 4 squares (total 16), the next size would be 5 x 5 squares totalling 25, which will in turn require extra yarn - and an adjustment in the number of stitches picked up for the border.

ABBREVIATIONS
See page 20.

SUGGESTED ALTERNATIVE COLOURWAYS

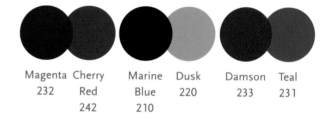

Magenta 232   Cherry Red 242   Marine Blue 210   Dusk 220   Damson 233   Teal 231

70 cm / 27 ½ in

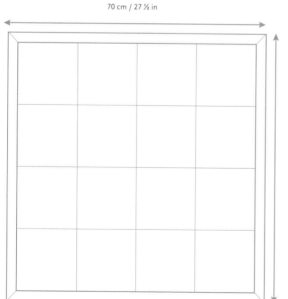

70 cm / 27 ½ in

TO MAKE (make 16)

With 5mm (US 8) needles and A leaving 30cm/12in for sewing up cast on 32 sts.
Beg with a k row work in st st and stripes of 6 rows A, [6 rows B, 6 rows A] 3 times.
Leaving 30cm/12in for sewing up cast off.

TO MAKE UP

Alternating the direction of the stripes, make up the squares to form a blanket 4 squares wide by 4 squares deep.
Edging (work 4 sides separately)
With right side facing, using 4mm (US 6) needles and A, pick up and k114 sts along side.
1st row K to end.
2nd row K1, m1, k to last st, m1, k1.
Rep the last 2 rows 3 times more.
Cast off.
Join row ends to form mitres.

66

MONA CARDIGAN

SKILL LEVEL Beginner / Improving

SIZES / MEASUREMENTS

To fit age	0-3	3-6	6-12	12-24	24-48*	48-72*	mths

ACTUAL GARMENT MEASUREMENTS

Chest	53	56	60	64	71	77	cm
	21	22	23 ½	25	28	30 ½	in
Length to	25	29	31	36	40	44	cm
back neck	9 ¾	11 ½	12 ¼	14	15 ¾	17 ½	in
Sleeve	14	16	18	21	24	28	cm
length	5 ½	6 ¼	7	8 ¼	9 ½	11	in

MATERIALS

- 10(10:11:12:13:13) 50g/1 ¾oz balls of MillaMia Naturally Soft Aran in Dusk (220).
- Pair each of 4mm (US 6) and 4.5mm (US 7) knitting needles.
- 8(8:8:10:10:10) buttons approx 15mm/½in in diameter for smaller sizes, approx 21mm/¾in in diameter for larger sizes.

TENSION / GAUGE

18 sts and 40 rows to 10cm/4in square over g- st using 4.5mm (US 7) needles.

HINTS AND TIPS

This stylish double breasted cardigan is knitted entirely in garter stitch making it the perfect, warm and cosy cover-up for brisk autumn mornings. The pockets are a fun design feature but could be omitted for the very smallest size or if you are a beginner knitter attempting a simple garment for the first time.

* The larger sizes can be worn as overcoats at the younger end of the age spectrum and as cardigans towards the upper end.

ABBREVIATIONS

See page 20.

SUGGESTED ALTERNATIVE COLOURWAYS

Damson	Teal	Cinder	Pink Glaze	Stone
233	231	201	223	202

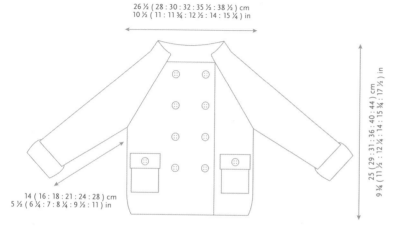

26 ½ (28 : 30 : 32 : 35 ½ : 38 ½) cm
10 ½ (11 : 11 ¾ : 12 ½ : 14 : 15 ¼) in

25 (29 : 31 : 36 : 40 : 44) cm
9 ¾ (11 ½ : 12 ¼ : 14 : 15 ¾ : 17 ½) in

14 (16 : 18 : 21 : 24 : 28) cm
5 ½ (6 ¼ : 7 : 8 ¼ : 9 ½ : 11) in

69

BACK

With 4.5mm (US 7) needles cast on 46(49:50:54:58:64) sts.
K 3 rows.
Inc row (right side) K3, m1, k to last 3 sts, m1, k3.
Rep the last 4 rows 1(1:2:2:3:3) times more.
50(53:56:60:66:72) sts.
Cont in g-st until back measures 13(15:17:20:23:26)cm/
5(6:6 ¾:8:10 ¼)in from cast on edge, ending with a
wrong side row.
Shape armholes
Cast off 4 sts at beg of next 2 rows. 42(45:48:52:56:64) sts.
1st, 2nd, 3rd, 4th and 5th sizes only
Next row K3(3:3:4:4:-), skpo, k to last 5(5:5:6:6:-) sts, k2 tog,
k3(3:3:4:4:-).
K 5 rows.
Rep the last 6 rows 1(2:2:4:2:-) times more.
38(39:42:42:50:-) sts.
All sizes
Next row K3(3:3:4:4:4), skpo, k to last 5(5:5:6:6:6) sts, k2 tog,
k3(3:3:4:4:4).
K 3 rows.
Rep the last 4 rows 8(8:9:7:11:17) times more.
20(21:22:26:26:28) sts.
Mark each end of last row with a coloured thread.
K7(7:9:9:11:11) rows.
Cast off.

LEFT FRONT

With 4.5mm (US 7) needles cast on 33(35:36:38:41:46) sts.
K 3 rows.
Inc row (right side) K3, m1, k to end.
Rep the last 4 rows 1(1:2:2:3:3) times more.
35(37:39:41:45:50) sts.
Cont in g-st until front measures 13(15:17:20:23:26)cm/
5(6:6 ¾:8:10 ¼)in from cast on edge, ending with a
wrong side row.
Shape armhole
Next row Cast off 4 sts, k to end. 31(33:35:37:41:46) sts.
K 1 row.
1st, 2nd, 3rd, 4th and 5th sizes only
Next row K3(3:3:4:4:-) skpo, k to end.
K 5 rows.
Rep the last 6 rows 1(2:2:4:2:-) times more.
29(30:32:32:38:-) sts.

All sizes

Next row K3(3:3:4:4:4) skpo, k to end.
K 3 rows.
Rep the last 4 rows 8(8:9:7:11:17) times more.
20(21:22:24:26:28) sts.
Cast off.
Mark position for buttons, the first pair 6 rows below cast off
edge, the 3rd(3rd:3rd:4th:4th:4th) pair 10(10:12:12:14:14)cm/
4(4:4 ¾:4 ¾:5 ½:5 ½)in from cast on edge and the remaining
1(1:1:2:2:2) pairs spaced evenly between.

RIGHT FRONT

With 4.5mm (US 7) needles cast on 33(35:36:38:41:46) sts.
K 3 rows.
Inc row (right side) K to last 3 sts, m1, k3.
Rep the last 4 rows 1(1:2:2:3:3) times more.
35(37:39:41:45:50) sts.
Cont in g-st until front measures 10(10:12:12:14:14)cm/
4(4:4 ¾:4 ¾:5 ½:5 ½)in from cast on edge, ending with a
wrong side row.
Buttonhole row K2, k2 tog, yf, k12(13:14:16:18:20), yf, skpo,
k to end.
Work remaining pairs of buttonholes to match.
Cont in g-st until front measures 13(15:17:20:23:26)cm/
5(6:6 ¾:8:10 ¼)in from cast on edge, ending with
a right side row.
Shape armhole
Next row Cast off 4 sts, k to end. 31(33:35:37:41:46) sts.
1st, 2nd, 3rd, 4th and 5th sizes only
Next row K to last 5(5:5:6:6:-) sts, k2 tog, k3(3:3:4:4:-).
K 5 rows.
Rep the last 6 rows 1(2:2:4:2:-) times more.
29(30:32:32:38:-) sts.
All sizes
Next row K to last 5(5:5:6:6:6) sts, k2 tog, k3(3:3:4:4:4).
K 3 rows.
Rep the last 4 rows 8(8:9:7:11:17) times more.
20(21:22:24:26:28) sts.
Cast off.

SLEEVES

With 4.5mm (US 7) needles cast on 27(30:33:36:39:42) sts.
K 13(13:15:15:17:17) rows.
Change to 4mm (US 6) needles.
Mark each end of last row with a coloured thread for cuffs.
K 13(13:15:15:17:17) rows.
Change to 4.5mm (US 7) needles.
K 3(3:5:5:7:7) rows.
Inc row K3, m1, k to last 3 sts, m1, k3.
K 7 rows.
Rep the last 8 rows 2(3:4:5:6:7) times more and then the inc
row again. 35(40:45:50:55:60) sts.
Cont straight until sleeve measures 14(16:18:21:24:28)cm/
5 ½(6 ¼:7:8 ¼:9 ½:11)in from coloured threads, ending with a
wrong side row.
Shape sleeve top
Cast off 4 sts at beg of next 2 rows. 27(32:37:42:47:52) sts.
1st and 2nd sizes only
Next row K3, skpo, k to last 5 sts, k2 tog, k3.
K 7 rows.
Rep the last 8 rows 5(2:-:-:-:-) times more.
15(26:-:-:-:-) sts.
2nd, 3rd, 4th, 5th and 6th sizes only
Next row K-(3:3:4:4:4) skpo, k to last -(5:5:6:6:6) sts, k2 tog,
k-(3:3:4:4:4).
K 5 rows.
Rep the last 6 rows -(4:8:6:4:3) times more.
-(16:19:28:37:44) sts.
3rd, 4th, 5th and 6th sizes only
Next row K-(-:3:4:4:4) skpo, k to last -(-:5:6:6:6) sts, k2 tog,
k-(-:3:4:4:4).
K 3 rows.
Rep the last 4 rows -(-:0:4:8:11) times more.
-(-:17:18:19:20) sts.
All sizes
Mark each end of last row with a coloured thread.
K7(7:9:9:11:11) rows.
Cast off.

POCKETS (make 2)

With 4.5mm (US 7) needles cast on 12(12:14:14:16:16) sts.
K 38(38:40:40:44:44) rows.
Buttonhole row K4(4:5:5:6:6), k2 tog, yf, k6(6:7:7:8:8).
K 4 rows.
Cast off.

TO MAKE UP

Matching coloured threads on top of sleeves to those on
back neck, join back raglan seams. Matching coloured
threads on top of sleeves to front cast off edges, join front
raglan seams. Join side and sleeve seams, reversing seams
for cuffs. Join under arm seams. Fold last 13 rows of pocket
to right side and sew to fronts. Sew on buttons.

FOLK CUSHION

SKILL LEVEL **Beginner / Improving**

SIZE

To fit a 35cm/13 ¾in by 35cm/13 ¾in cushion pad.

MATERIALS

- Three 50g/1 ¾oz balls of MillaMia Naturally Soft Aran in Powder Blue (222) (M).
- One ball in Ivory (221) (C).
- Pair of 5mm (US 8) knitting needles.
- 5 buttons approx 21mm/¾in in diameter.

TENSION / GAUGE

18 sts and 24 rows to 10cm/4in square over st st using 5mm (US 8) needles.

HINTS AND TIPS

This stunning cushion with its simple, repeating motif is a great project to try knitting Fairisle for the first time as there is no shaping to contend with at the same time. Co-ordinate it to the child's bedroom colour scheme for a fun comfy accessory, or why not knit it as an unusual, thoughtful gift for a new baby? To mix things up you can always start a second cushion on row 21 as opposed to row 1 of the Chart - as we have done in our Powder Blue version.

ABBREVIATIONS

See page 20.

NOTE

When working from Chart odd numbered rows are k rows and read from right to left. Even numbered rows are p rows and read from left to right.

Use the Fairisle method, strand the yarn not in use across the wrong side of work weaving them under and over the working yarn every 3 or 4 sts.

SUGGESTED ALTERNATIVE COLOURWAYS

Powder Blue 222   Ivory 221   Cinder 201   Ivory 221   Marine Blue 210   Latte 203

34 ½ cm / 13 ½ in

34 ½ cm / 13 ½ in

FRONT

Using 5mm (US 8) needles and M cast on 62 sts.
Beg with a k row cont in st st and patt.
Work 2 rows M, 2 rows C.
Work from Chart.
1st row K3M, [work across 1st row of 28 st patt rep] twice, k3M.
2nd row P3M, [work across 2nd row of 28 st patt rep] twice, p3M.
These 2 rows set the Chart.
3rd to 40th rows Cont in patt to end of Chart row 40.
41st to 80th rows Rep 1st to 40th rows again.
Work 2 rows M. Cast off.

BACK

Lower back
Using 5mm (US 8) needles and M cast on 62 sts.
Beg with a k row work 59 rows in st st.
Cut off M.
Join on C.
Next row P to end.
1st rib row K5, [p4, k4] to last 9 sts, p4, k5.
2nd rib row P5, [k4, p4] to last 9 sts, k4, p5.
Rep the last 2 rows twice more.
Cast off in rib.

Upper back
Using 5mm (US 8) needles and C cast on 62 sts.
1st rib row K5, [p4, k4] to last 9 sts, p4, k5.
2nd rib row P5, [k4, p4] to last 9 sts, k4, p5.
Work 1 more row.
Buttonhole row Rib 6, [rib2 tog, yrn, rib 10] 4 times, rib2 tog, yrn, rib 6.
Rib 2 more rows.
Cut off C.
Join on M.
Beg with a k row work 20 rows in st st.
Cast off.

TO MAKE UP

Back: Lay upper back over lower back and tack in place. With right sides together, sew back to front. Turn to right side, sew on buttons.
Insert cushion pad.

CHART

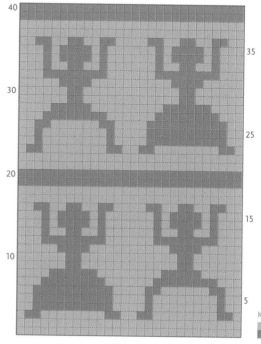

Key
Pink Glaze (223) (M)
Latte (203) (C)

76

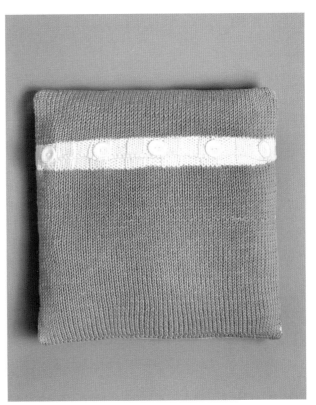

MOSES CABLE PANTS

SKILL LEVEL **Improving**

SIZES / MEASUREMENTS

To fit age	0-3	3-6	6-12	12-18	18-24	mths

ACTUAL GARMENT MEASUREMENTS

Around	36	40	44	49	53	cm
nappy	14	16	17 ½	19 ½	21	in
Length	25	28	31	35	39	cm
	10	11	12 ¼	13 ¾	15 ¼	in

MATERIALS

- 3 (3:4:4:5) 50g/1 ¾oz balls of MillaMia Naturally Soft Aran in Powder Blue (222).
- Pair each of 4mm (US 6) and 5mm (US 8) knitting needles.
- Cable needle.
- Waist length of elastic.

TENSION / GAUGE

18 sts and 24 rows to 10cm/4in square over st st using 5mm (US 8) needles.

HINTS AND TIPS

These knitted trousers are the height of comfort for baby. Elasticated at the waist to ensure that they stay on over a nappy, and with plenty of room in the legs, these comfy pants allow for ease of movement while keeping an active baby toasty warm.

ABBREVIATIONS

C4F, cable 4 front - slip next 2 sts on a cable needle and hold at front of work, k2, then k2 from cable needle.
C4B, cable 4 back - slip next 2 sts on a cable needle and hold at back of work, k2, then k2 from cable needle.
See also page 20.

SUGGESTED ALTERNATIVE COLOURWAYS

Latte	Damson	Teal	Ochre	Stone
203	233	231	240	202

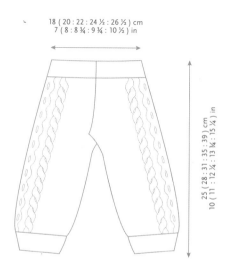

18 (20 : 22 : 24 ½ : 26 ½) cm
7 (8 : 8 ¾ : 9 ¾ : 10 ½) in

25 (28 : 31 : 35 : 39) cm
10 (11 : 12 ¼ : 13 ¾ : 15 ¼) in

LEGS (both alike)

With 4mm (US 6) needles cast on 40(44:48:52:56) sts.
Rib row [K1, p1] to end.
Work a further 9 rows.
Change to 5mm (US 8) needles.
1st row K8(10:12:14:16), p2, k4, p2, k8, p2, k4, p2,
k8(10:12:14:16).
2nd row P to end.
3rd row K8(10:12:14:16), p2, C4F, p2, C4B, C4F, p2, C4B, p2,
k8(10:12:14:16).
4th row P to end.
5th and 6th rows As 1st and 2nd rows.
7th row K8(10:12:14:16), p2, C4F, p2, C4F, C4B, p2, C4B, p2,
k8(10:12:14:16).
8th row row P to end.
These 8 rows form the patt.
Cont in patt until work measures 11(12:14:15:17)cm/
4 ¼(4 ¾:5 ½:6:6 ¾)in from cast on edge, ending with a p row.
Shape crotch
Inc row K2, m1, patt to last 2 sts, m1, k2.
Next row P to end.
Rep the last 2 rows 3(3:4:4:5) times more.
48(52:58:62:68) sts.
Cast on 3(3:3:4:4) sts at beg of next 2 rows.
54(58:64:70:76) sts.
Shape for legs
Work 2 rows.
Next row K2, skpo, patt to last 4 sts, k2 tog, k2.
Next row P to end.
Rep the last 2 rows 3(3:4:5:5) times more. 46(50:54:58:64) sts.
Cont straight until work measures 23(27:29:33:37)cm/
9(10 ½:11 ½:13:14 ½)in from cast on edge, ending
with a p row.
Change to 4mm (US 6) needles.
Work 10 rows in rib.
Cast off in rib.

TO MAKE UP

Join inner leg seams. Join centre front and back seam. Join elastic into a ring. Work a herringbone casing over rib at waist, enclosing elastic.

BOSSE CARDIGAN

SKILL LEVEL **Improving**

SIZES / MEASUREMENTS

To fit age	6-12	12-18	24-36	48-60	mths

ACTUAL GARMENT MEASUREMENTS

Chest	62	65	73	77	cm
	24 ½	25 ½	28 ½	30 ½	in
Length	28	32	36	40	cm
to shoulder	11	12 ½	14 ¼	15 ¾	in
Sleeve length	18	21	25	28	cm
	7	8 ¼	10	11	in

MATERIALS

- 5(6:6:7) 50g/1 ¾oz balls of MillaMia Naturally Soft Aran in Marine Blue (210).
- Pair each of 4mm (US 6) and 5mm (US 8) knitting needles.
- Circular 4mm (US 6) knitting needle.
- 4 buttons approx 21mm/¾in in diameter.

TENSION / GAUGE

21 sts and 28 rows to 10cm/4in square over patt using 5mm (US 8) needles.

HINTS AND TIPS

This sweet cardigan is simple in its shaping and rich in texture. The twisted moss stitch adds interest for the knitter as well as providing a snug fabric that will ensure this cardi can equally double up as a light winter jacket. Short row shaping gives the collar its nice shape.

ABBREVIATIONS

See also page 20.

SUGGESTED ALTERNATIVE COLOURWAYS

Powder Blue 222	Damson 233	Teal 231	Cinder 201	Emerald 241

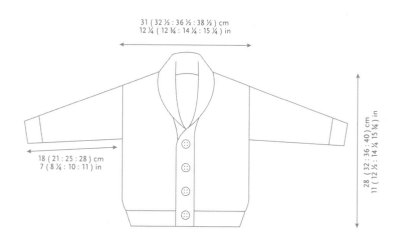

31 (32 ½ : 36 ½ : 38 ½) cm
12 ¼ (12 ¾ : 14 ¼ : 15 ¼) in

18 (21 : 25 : 28) cm
7 (8 ¼ : 10 : 11) in

28 (32 : 36 : 40) cm
11 (12 ½ : 14 ¼ 15 ¾) in

BACK

With 4mm (US 6) needles cast on 67(71:79:83) sts.
1st rib row P1, [k1, p1] to end.
2nd rib row K1, [p1, k1] to end.
Rep the last 2 rows 3(4:4:5) times more.
Change to 5mm (US 8) needles.
1st row P1, [k1tbl, p1] to end.
2nd row K to end.
These 2 rows form the patt.
Cont in patt until back measures 17(20:23:26)cm/
6 ¾(8:9:10 ¼)in from cast on edge, ending with a k row.
Shape armholes
Cast off 3(3:4:4) sts at beg of next 2 rows. 61(65:71:75) sts.
Cont in patt until back measures 28(32:36:40)cm/
11(12 ½:14 ¼:15 ¾)in from cast on edge, ending with a k row.
Shape shoulders
Cast off 5 sts at beg of next 2 rows, 7(7:8:9) sts at beg of next 2
rows and 7(8:9:9) sts at beg of foll 2 rows. 23(25:27:29) sts.
Cast off.

LEFT FRONT

With 4mm (US 6) needles cast on 29(31:35:37) sts.
1st rib row P1, [k1, p1] to end.
2nd rib row K1, [p1, k1] to end.
Rep the last 2 rows 3(4:4:5) times more.
Change to 5mm (US 8) needles.
1st row P1, [k1tbl, p1] to end.
2nd row K to end.
These 2 rows form the patt.
Cont in patt until front measures 17(20:23:26)cm/
6 ¾(8:9:10 ¼)in from cast on edge, ending with a k row.
Shape armhole and front neck
Next row Cast off 3(3:4:4) sts, patt to last 2 sts, work 2 tog.
Work 3 rows.
Next row Patt to last 2 sts, work 2 tog.
Rep the last 4 rows until 19(20:22:23) sts rem.
Work straight until front measures the same as back to
shoulder, ending at armhole edge.
Shape shoulder
Cast off 5 sts at beg of next row, 7(7:8:9) sts at beg of foll
right side row.
Work 1 row.
Cast off rem 7(8:9:9) sts.

RIGHT FRONT

With 4mm (US 6) needles cast on 29(31:35:37) sts.
1st rib row P1, [k1, p1] to end.
2nd rib row K1, [p1, k1] to end.
Rep the last 2 rows 3(4:4:5) times more.
Change to 5mm (US 8) needles.
1st row P1, [k1tbl, p1] to end.
2nd row K to end.
These 2 rows form the patt.
Cont in patt until front measures 17(20:23:26)cm/
6 ¾(8:9:10 ¼) in from cast on edge, ending with a k row.
Shape armhole and front neck
Next row Skpo, patt to end.
Next row Cast off 3(3:4:4) sts, patt to end.
Work 2 rows.
Next row Skpo, patt to end.
Work 3 rows.
Next row Skpo, patt to end.
Rep the last 4 rows until 19(20:22:23) sts rem.
Work straight until front measures the same as back to
shoulder, ending at armhole edge.
Shape shoulder
Cast off 5 sts at beg of next row, 7(7:8:9) sts at beg of
foll wrong side row.
Work 1 row.
Cast off rem 7(8:9:9) sts.

SLEEVES

With 4mm (US 6) needles cast on 31(33:35:37) sts.
1st rib row P1, [k1, p1] to end.
2nd rib row K1, [p1, k1] to end.
Rep the last 2 rows 3(4:4:5) times more.
Change to 5mm (US 8) needles.
1st row P1, [k1tbl, p1] to end.
2nd row K to end.
These 2 rows form the patt.
Work 2 rows.
Inc row Inc in first st, patt to last 2 sts, inc in next st, patt 1.
Work 3 rows.
Rep the last 4 rows 5(6:8:9) times more and then the inc row again. 45(49:55:59) sts.
Cont straight until sleeve measures 18(21:25:28)cm/
7(8 ¼:10:11)in from cast on edge, ending with a k row.
Shape sleeve top
Cast off 3(3:4:4) sts at beg of next 2 rows. 39(43:47:51) sts
Cast off 2 sts at beg of 10(10:12:12) rows.
Cast off.

LEFT FRONT BAND and COLLAR

With 4mm (US 6) circular needle, cast on 17(19:21:23) sts, with right side facing, pick up and k25(27:29:31) sts from shoulder to beg of neck shaping, 37(43:49:55) sts to cast on edge.
79(89:99:109) sts.
1st row P1, [k1, p1] to end.
This row sets the rib.
Next 2 rows Rib 16(18:20:22), turn, rib to end.
Next 2 rows Rib 20(22:24:26), turn, rib to end.
Next 2 rows Rib 24(26:28:30), turn, rib to end.
Cont in this way for a further 12(16:16:18) rows work 4 more sts on every alt row.
Work 5 rows across all sts.
Buttonhole row Rib 2, rib 2 tog, yrn, [rib 8(10:12:14), rib2 tog, yrn] 3 times, rib to end.
Rib a further 5 rows.
Cast off in rib.

RIGHT FRONT BAND and COLLAR

With 4mm (US 6) circular needle and right side facing, pick up and k37(43:49:55) sts to beg of neck shaping, 25(27:29:31) sts to shoulder, cast on 17(19:21:23) sts.
79(89:99:109) sts.
Working in rib as given for left front band and collar, work as folls:
Next 2 rows Rib16(18:20:22), turn, rib to end.
Next 2 rows Rib 20(22:24:26), turn, rib to end.
Next 2 rows Rib 24(26:28:30), turn, rib to end.
Cont in this way for a further 12(16:16:18) rows work 4 more sts on every alt row.
Work 12 rows across all sts.
Cast off in rib.

TO MAKE UP

Join collar and sew to back neck edge. Join side and sleeve seams. Sew in sleeves. Sew on buttons.

TOMAS TANK TOP

SKILL LEVEL **Beginner / Improving**

SIZES / MEASUREMENTS

To fit age	3-6	6-12	12-24	24-36	36-48	48-60	mths

ACTUAL GARMENT MEASUREMENTS

Chest	40	44	48	56	60	68	cm
	15 ½	17 ½	19	22	23 ½	26 ¾	in
Length to	25	27	30	33	37	41	cm
shoulder	10	10 ½	11 ¾	13	14 ½	16	in

MATERIALS

Two colour version
• 2(3:3:4:4:5) 50g/1 ¾oz balls of MillaMia Naturally Soft Aran in Powder Blue (222) (M).
• One ball in Ivory (221) (C).

One colour version
• 2(3:3:4:4:5) 50g/1 ¾oz balls of MillaMia Naturally Soft Aran in Ivory (221).

All versions
• Pair each of 4mm (US 6) and 5mm (US 8) knitting needles.

TENSION / GAUGE

20 sts and 30 rows to 10cm/4in square over patt using 5mm (US 8) needles.

HINTS AND TIPS

Small babies in large textured knits are always so appealing, and this tank top in our new Aran weight yarn knits up in a trice. Choose subtle colours for a muted, baby soft look or go for bright and bold to make a daring statement!

ABBREVIATIONS

See page 20.

SUGGESTED ALTERNATIVE COLOURWAYS

Cobalt	Stone	Damson	Marine Blue	Latte	Ivory
230	202	233	210	203	221

20 (22 : 24 : 28 : 30 : 34) cm
7 ¾ (8 ¾ : 9 ½ : 11 : 11 ¾ : 13 ½) in

25 (27 : 30 : 33 : 37 : 41) cm
10 (10 ½ : 11 ¾ : 13 : 14 ½ : 16) in

BACK

With 4mm (US 6) needles and C, cast on 42(46:50:58:62:70) sts.
1st rib row K2, [p2, k2] to end.
2nd rib row P2, [k2, p2] to end.
Rep the last 2 rows 2(2:3:3:4:4) times more and then the first row again.
Change to 5mm (US 8) needles and M.
Next row P to end.
1st row K2, [p2, k2] to end.
2nd row P2, [k2, p2] to end.
3rd row P2, [k2, p2] to end.
4th row K2, [p2, k2] to end.
These 4 rows form the double moss st.
Work straight until back measures 15(16:18:20:23:26)cm/
6(6 ¼:7:8:9:10 ¼)in from cast on edge, ending with
a wrong side row.
Shape armholes
Cast off 4(4:4:5:5:5) sts at beg of next 2 rows.
34(38:42:48:52:60) sts **.
Next row Skpo, patt to last 2 sts, k2 tog.
Next row Patt to end.
Rep the last 2 rows 2(3:4:5:5:7) times. 28(30:32:36:40:44) sts.
Cont in patt until back measures 25(27:30:33:37:41)cm/
10(10 ½:11 ¾:13:14 ½:16)in from cast on edge, ending with a
wrong side row.
Shape shoulders
Cast off 5(5:5:5:7:7) sts at beg of next 2 rows.
18(20:22:26:26:30) sts.
Leave these sts on a holder.

FRONT

Work as given for back to **.
Shape front neck
Next row Skpo, patt 12(14:16:19:21:25), k2 tog, turn and work
on these sts for first side of front neck.
Next row Patt to end.
Next row Skpo patt to last 2 sts, k2 tog.
Rep the last 2 rows 2(3:4:5:5:7) times. 8(8:8:9:11:11) sts.
Keeping armhole edge straight cont to dec at neck edge on
3(3:3:4:4:4) foll 4th rows. 5(5:5:5:7:7) sts.
Cont straight until front measures same as back to shoulder,
ending at armhole edge.
Shape shoulder
Cast off.
With right side facing, slip centre 2 sts onto a safety pin, join on
yarn to rem sts.

Next row Skpo patt to last 2 sts, k2 tog.
Next row Patt to end.
Next row Skpo patt to last 2 sts, k2 tog.
Rep the last 2 rows 2(3:4:5:5:7) times. 8(8:8:9:11:11) sts.
Keeping armhole edge straight cont to dec at neck edge on
3(3:3:4:4:4) foll 4th rows. 5(5:5:5:7:7) sts.
Cont straight until front measures same as back to shoulder,
ending at armhole edge.
Shape shoulder
Cast off.

NECKBAND

Join right shoulder seam.
With right side facing, using 4mm (US 6) needles and
C, pick up and k24(26:30:32:36:40) sts evenly down
left side of front neck, k2 from safety pin, pick up and
k22(26:28:30:34:38) sts evenly up right side of front
neck, k18(20:22:26:26:30) sts from back neck holder.
66(74:82:90:98:110) sts.
1st, 4th, 5th and 6th sizes only
1st row P2, [k2, p2] to end.
2nd and 3rd and 4th sizes only
1st row K2, [p2, k2] to end.
All sizes
This row sets the rib.
2nd row Rib 23(25:29:31:35:39), k2 tog, skpo, rib to end.
3rd row Rib to end.
Cast off in rib, dec on this row as before.

ARMBANDS

Join left shoulder seam and neckband.
With right side facing, using 4mm (US 6) needles and C,
pick up and k66(70:74:82:86:90) sts evenly around armhole
edge.
1st row P2, [k2, p2] to end.
2nd row K2, [p2, k2] to end.
These 2 rows set the rib patt.
Work 1 more row.
Cast off in rib.

TO MAKE UP

Join side and armband seams.

YARN COLOURS

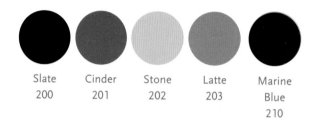

Slate
200

Cinder
201

Stone
202

Latte
203

Marine
Blue
210

Dusk
220

Ivory
221

Powder
Blue
222

Pink Glaze
223

Cobalt
230

Teal
231

Magenta
232

Damson
233

Ochre
240

Emerald
241

Cherry
Red
242

NOTES

INDEX

JENS JUMPER
page 58

FREJA BLANKET
page 64

MONA CARDIGAN
page 68

FOLK CUSHION
page 74

MOSES CABLE PANTS
page 78

BOSSE CARDIGAN
page 82

TOMAS TANK TOP
page 88

ABOUT MILLAMIA

A new yarn line at last. Something our customers had been asking us for again and again, and in the end we felt we really had to listen! It took us a little while but we hope you will agree it has been worth the wait.

With the luxury of going back to the drawing board and starting from scratch, we took our time thinking about what would be the best next step for MillaMia. A totally new fibre? A new colour palette? A new weight? There are lots of variables to consider when it comes to yarn after all.

We decided to ask you, our customers, what you wanted. We conducted surveys at some of our retail shows. We spoke to our stockists to see what they would like to see more of, and where they would like us to expand. We had the fun of a few trips to Italy to visit mills and the famous Pitti Filati show in Florence. Inspiring - if a bit overwhelming at times.

In the end the answer seemed quite obvious. We knew that people loved knitting with MillaMia Naturally Soft Merino and we fervently believe in the qualities that we think make it a great yarn - especially for children's patterns. But we knew that lots of people also like a slightly thicker yarn for some projects. When you are in a hurry - for instance when Christmas is nearly upon you and the knitting gift list seems unfeasible, perhaps it is a large item, or when you want to make something for a newborn but the due date is just around the corner.

And so MillaMia Naturally Soft Aran was born. Combining all the qualities of Naturally Soft Merino that we loved - the extrafine merino composition, the super soft handle, the fabulous stitch definition and the machine washabiity - but in an Aran gauge. As far as we were able we replicated the tight twist that our yarn is known for, but knew we would have to loosen it slightly, so that you end up with lightweight, wearable knits. We are thrilled with the results.

Helena was not content to simply copy our existing palette however. Instead as she knew she also wanted to use Naturally Soft Aran for adult knits (watch this space - coming soon!), she introduced a small core of melanges, and enjoyed custom defining the other twelve solid colours. As ever we had lots of back and forth to the mill until Helena was fully satisfied, but the end result was well worth the work. A super collection of toning and deliberately clashing shades that look beautiful together. We hope all of you will also enjoy playing with these new colours.

When it then came to thinking about pattern support it felt totally natural that our first collection should be one for babies and children. After all that is what we first launched MillaMia with and is what people have always known us for. We have focused slightly more on the really young ones this time, which has been fun and inspiring. Although as it has been a while since we have worked on a kid's photoshoot we had forgotten some of the challenges of working with children!

We have been lucky as ever to be so well supported by friends and family, and friends of friends for our pictures. Not to mention our incredible test knitters who work to unbelievable deadlines to help us get all our colourways ready on time. The good news is that they all loved working with the new yarn - which we felt was praise indeed as they are as close to what we would call 'expert knitters' as anyone we know!

Please do let us know what you think - about the new yarn, our new colours and our new patterns. We love hearing from you and it makes all the hard work worthwhile.

With best wishes,

Katarina and Helena Rosén
katarina@millamia.com or helena@millamia.com